Seeing Life in the 1940s and '50s Through the Eyes of a Nebraska Child

You're a Good Man!
Bless you!
Darlene Hill

D1450934

DARLENE HILL

PAGE PUBLISHING, INC.
New York, NY

First originally published by Page Publishing, Inc. 2017

ISBN 978-1-64082-937-4 (Paperback)
ISBN 978-1-64082-938-1 (Digital)

Printed in the United States of America

CHAPTER 1

When I Was Born

I was born at home in Spalding, Nebraska, which is in Greeley County. I was delivered by Dr. Giever with the help of Gram Bartlett, an older lady that lived down the street from us. On this fine day of October 27, 1941, I was a lot of baby weighing in at twelve pounds. My mom was Margaret Naomi (Noonan) Marshall, and my dad was Roy Kenneth Marshall. When I got here I had a big brother, Roy Michael, who was ten years old, and a big sister, Margaret Jeannine, who was nine years old.

My mom told me that my daddy wasn't too happy when she got pregnant with me. Now at my age I know where he was coming from as he was forty-nine years old when I was born. I'm sure I wouldn't want to start another set of kids at that age.

I do know that Mom was happy to have me and my sister had prayed for a little sister for many years, so she was overjoyed. As far as my brother, I don't think he was too excited about babies.

Even though I was a cute little—or should I say big—baby, they all had to get pretty tired of me as they say I had a bad case of colic for some time. I guess Mom, Mike, and Nean took turns walking the floor with me. Daddy by this time had gotten over being upset about me and wanted so badly to hold me but my family said until I was six months old I wouldn't have a thing to do with him. I guess it was my way of getting even for him not wanting me at first. But you know, after we got that worked out, no one ever loved each other more than us.

Jeannine 10yrs   Darlene 9mos   Mike 11yrs

CHAPTER 2

About the House I Grew Up In

We lived in a three-bedroom house. It was the shape of a barn with a big porch that wrapped around the south and east side. There were two bedrooms and a bath upstairs. Yes, we had an inside bath, and most who lived in town had them. However, the farm folks still had the outhouse.

The south room was Mike's, which he later shared with Don. I'll tell you about him later. The north room was Nean's, which she shared with me. Just so you know, Nean was what I called my sister and still do.

The main floor had one bedroom, which was Mom's and Dad's, and it had one long narrow closet. Mom kept a curtain hanging in its doorway as it had no door.

Our kitchen had been built on the north side of the house, and it was about twelve feet wide and ten feet deep. There was one window on the west side, and it looked to be a regular window lying down and the window would slide open.

In our kitchen we had a wood-burning stove. Mom did all her baking and cooking on it, and it also helped heat the house in the winter. We used corncobs Dad got from a nearby farmer to start the stove. As I got older, it was my job to bring Mom in a basket of cobs to start her stove. Nean told about one time I was sent out to get cobs and when I didn't come back for a long time, Mom came out to check on me and I was counting every cob as I put them in the basket. Mom got a picture of that.

Since I mentioned pictures I'm going to take time here to tell you about pictures back then. To get a picture you had to own a camera, and we didn't have phones that you could take pictures with. The camera was a box shape that you had to buy film for so you could take a picture. You would load it into your camera and snap a picture, but if you didn't turn the film it would take another picture on top of the one you took, ruining both of them. The film had around twelve pictures you could take on a roll. Also to take a picture inside you had to use a flashbulb. Now flashbulbs came in a box of twelve I think. Anyway, you would have to have an attachment on your camera to put the bulb into. When you snapped a picture, a bright light would flash, which made enough light for you to get a good picture inside. With these cameras you never knew what your picture was going to look like until you sent the film into a company that would print them for you. Anyway, you will find a lot of the old pictures were taken outside because it was a lot cheaper than buying flashbulbs.

I think that my grandparents must have had some money as we have lots of snapshots of my mom and her brother when they were quite young. Most families only have pictures that some guy would take as he was traveling through the area, as they couldn't afford a camera. Mom took lots of pictures, which we all cherish today.

Well, back to the kitchen. Off the kitchen was a laundry room. Someone had enclosed part of the wraparound porch. It had a north window and an east window and an outside door. It worked really well in the summer, but in the winter with no heat, it was a cold place to work.

The dining room housed my mom's buffet and our round oak table that had leaves to extend it, probably sixteen to eighteen feet long. It was opened up many times when I was growing up. Mom loved to cook and bake, and back then families got together a lot more often.

Off the dining room was a pantry that held groceries, extra dishes, and large cooking pots and pans plus other odds and ends like the ironing board and iron. Dad made Mom's ironing board, and to prove how strong it was, he did a handstand on the very end of it.

Our living room was a pretty large room, with a big bay window on the south wall where Mom with her green thumb kept her flowers. When I was young, the north wall in the living room was open into the bedroom and had a curtain hanging for privacy. In later years, Dad put a wall in there. The east wall had an open stairway that turned at ceiling height and went on to the second floor. At the top were three doors. The north was our bedroom, the south was the boys', and straight in was the bathroom.

Also there was a big piano on the west wall of the living room. No one knew how to play, but Mom enjoyed trying. Sometimes someone would come that could play and we would all sing along and have a good old time.

This is where I was born & raised.
Dad's car after the '50 ford.
Taken the winter of 1963.

MOM WAS THE BEST COOK IN THE WHOLE WORLD. LOTS OF PEOPLE IN TOWN BOUGHT HER HOMEMADE BREAD. WHEN WE GOT HOME FROM SCHOOL A FRESH ROLL TASTED SO GOOD. THANKS MOM!!!!!!!

CHAPTER 3

About Our Yard

Our yard was quite big, but it was all hills. You would go east or north in our yard and it was uphill. You go west or south and it was downhill to the sidewalk and then downhill from the sidewalks to the street. It was a real pain to mow. Most of the yard was pretty much weeds, but we had to keep them mowed too. At that time there were no mowers with engines, as you pushed them a blade would turn and cut the grass. There were two large lilac bushes on the east side of the porch going up the little hill to the clothesline. That is where we buried all of our pets that died.

I have to stop here and tell you about the possums. Well, Mike or Dad brought them home because they had no parents. There were two of them, and they still had their eyes closed as they were just a few days old. Well, Mom washed up one of my doll's baby bottles and warmed milk for them, and it was Don's and my job to keep them fed. Well, things went well for a few days, but one day we went to feed them and they were rolled into a ball and wouldn't respond to nothing so we figured that they were dead and we buried them in our pet cemetery. To this day we aren't sure if they were dead or just playing possum.

Back to the yard. One year, Dad decided to take the lilac bushes out that left a big bare spot on the little hill. It finally filled in with weeds. One day when the folks were gone somewhere, Don and I took it upon ourselves to pull all the weeds that had taken over the bare spot. It took us a long time, but by the time the folks got home, we were finished and were so proud of ourselves. When we showed Dad, I could tell something was wrong. He never got upset. He just said, "It's going to take a while before the weeds come back so they can keep the hill from washing away."

My Mommy & Me
Fall of 1942

CHAPTER 4

Stories about Me When I Was Little

Of course, the first few years of my life I can't remember too well but my sister, Nean, told a lot of rather cute stories about me.

First of all I was spoiled rotten. From what I hear, Nean and Mike did that. Well anyway, my mom, like most moms back then, didn't work outside the home but she worked her buns off at home. She took in washing and ironing, and she also baked bread and sold it. Mike and Nean had the job of delivering it.

The lady that owned a local bar was a steady customer, and Nean would take me along when she delivered there. I was only two or three at the time, and everyone made a fuss over me. She said the guys at the bar would stand me up on a table and get me to sing and dance for them. I must have been cute, because then they would all give me money and Nean said lots of times I made more money on my little show than Mom made on her bread. Just think if my folks had been rich and I could have gotten my due publicity, I could have played Shirley Temple in the movies. Oh well, this won't be the last calling I'll miss in my lifetime.

I was just talking to my sister last night, and she was telling me about the time she had let me ride in her bicycle basket when she was sent downtown for something. I was two or three years old, and I just fit in the basket that was on the front of Nean's bike. Well, everything went well until we got almost to the store. Then she hit a small stone and it tipped us over. She said that she jumped up and checked me over and I didn't have a scratch, plus I was smiling. I was probably thinking this was a new game and I liked it. When she finally took time to look at herself, she found she had a leg full of gravel. She took me and went across the street where the lady she worked for picked the gravel out of her leg and got it all doctored up. She always put me first and took very good care of me.

Another thing she told me about was when she took me in the drug store, which had a soda and ice cream bar. She sat me up to the bar and asked which I wanted, an ice cream cone or a soda. It seemed like Mom had given her ten cents so we could both get a treat. Well, like I said, I was really spoiled. I told her I wanted both and I wouldn't change my mind. Well, she let me have my way and sat there and watched me enjoy my treat and hers. I was about three or four years old then.

Something else she told me about was when I was born I had no hair and I guess it took forever to come in. Nean said that it came in straight and pretty thin. When I was around three, Nean and Mom decided to give me a home perm. All went well, and when they took out the rollers, I had little curls all over my head. They took me out in front of the house and got a picture of them, and then they proceeded to rinse the stuff out like the directions called for. When they rinsed it out, all the curls were gone. It's a good thing they got a picture first as that's all they got out of the whole afternoon's work.

Also Nean told about the time she woke up in the night and could hear me counting one, two, three, and on up. She got up looking for me and found me sitting on the dresser Dad made me, counting the stars. I had been sticking gold stars that I got in Sunday school on the mirror every week. Nean said I was sound asleep, I had pulled out the dresser drawers and crawled up on them. I guess I didn't even wake up when she put me back to bed. She said I was around three then.

These are the curls from my home pern that washed out.

CHAPTER 5

About Church

We went to the First Presbyterian Church nearly every Sunday. The only other church was the Catholic church, and most of the town went there. I can still remember getting all dressed up for church and then the whole family would walk two blocks south, one block east, and then another block south. My sister told about the time I sang in church. It seemed that "Pistol Packin' Mama" was a very popular song on the radio at that time. Well anyway, when everyone got up to sing I stood up in the pew and sang my song. I sang "Pissy packy mama" because I was only about two years old, and everyone but my folks thought it was cute. I must have gotten a good talking to as they say I never sang that song in church again.

This was the church I was baptized in, married in, and two of my children were baptized here also. Some of my memories at church were Sunday school, which was after church services. I got many pins for having a perfect attendance. In the summer we had Bible school for two weeks, and we'd be there all day. Parents would bring in lunch and treats. We'd learn Bible verses and new songs and also do a lot of crafts. It was a lot of fun, and we had a program on the last day so we could show everyone all we had learned and what we had made.

Then there was the Ladies Aid Society. This was all the ladies of the church, and they would get together once or twice a month, have a meeting, plan church socials, and such. After all was taken care of, they would sit around a quilt frame quilting. This really left an impression on me. I would sit on the floor at Mom's feet and play with other kids that were there, and it was a constant buzz as our moms talked the afternoon away.

Speaking of church socials, everyone took part. Some of the food was cooked at the church, but the salads, bread, pies, and such were all donated. One thing that sticks out in my memory was the pie room. First, I should tell you the dinners took place in the church basement where there was a large social room, a kitchen, the restrooms, and a Sunday school room that opened up to the big room so it could be used for overflow. Then there was this long narrow room with shelves on both sides.

This room was called the pie room, and the ladies would set all the pies in there, cut them, and serve them as needed. It was quite a sight when you are little to see a whole room full of pies. Of course, like everything else the room shrunk as I got older.

Back then, Sundays were special. Hardly no one worked because all the stores were closed. Therefore, you couldn't go shopping either, so after church, we had someone over for dinner or we would go to someone else's house, have dinner, and spend the afternoon visiting. As for us kids we would enjoy playing all day.

Presbyterian Church Spalding.

CHAPTER 6

Don Coming into the Picture

I guess it's about time to tell you about Don. Just one day before my third birthday, Mom had a baby boy, and they named him Donald Eugene. Needless to say, I wasn't a bit happy about him. I was perfectly happy being the baby of the family and I sure wasn't ready to share. Oh well, I could see that they weren't going to send him back so I guess I'd just have to put up with him. As I look back, I remember some good times we had and we had our share of fighting, but we both survived.

Darlene & Donnie Marshall

CHAPTER 7

Things Our Family Did

Some of the things we did as I was growing up that stuck in my mind are we all sat down around the oak table with clawed feet, and ate our evening meal together. We had no TV, but back then no one did. However, we had a radio and at 6:30 p.m. the *Lone Ranger* came on and we got to listen to it as we ate. Well, the thing I remember about supper was when Dad would empty his coffee cup, he would take it to the kitchen and fill it up, and bring the coffee pot back to the dining room and say, "Chock yourselves," meaning of course, if you want any more coffee, be ready. It got to be as soon as Dad got up to get coffee someone would say, "Chock yourselves." We always ate at the oak table for supper as most of the time all six of us were home for that meal. We had a small table in the kitchen that Mom used when she was baking and it worked well if there were only three or four of us eating.

Something else we would do was in the summer when it was so hot Dad would take us for a ride in the car after supper to cool off. There was no air conditioner in the car, so we would have all the windows open to cool us off as we rode around the country. It didn't matter if you drove the country roads or the highways as none of them were paved back then, whichever road we took we had a lot of dust to cope with, but it was better than the heat. Once in a while we would see a lone deer. That was exciting as there weren't that many of them in Nebraska back then. We always saw a lot of rabbits, some prairie dogs, and of course, coons and skunks. If we were really lucky, Dad would stop at Fox's Drug Store, which had a drive-in window, where you could get ice cream and sodas. That was a real treat and the cold ice cream helped cool us down.

Talking about air conditioning, no one I knew had it in their house. I guess it wasn't invented yet, but we had a fan (one fan, not one for every room). Mom would set it on a chair facing the back of the chair where she would hang a wet towel. As the fan blew through it, it would help cool a room, not too much, but everything helped.

Those of you who are reading this, think about how well off you have it today. If you were to go back further in time it was much harder living then when I grew up, and people had to be really tough to live through all they did than when you are complaining about how hard you have to work or many other things we complain about, just stop and think about how really easy you have it now.

CHAPTER 8

Going To Uncle George's

I can remember going to Uncle George and Aunt Mary's many times. Uncle George was Mom's brother, and they lived with Grandpa Noonan, Mom's dad. They lived on the farm where Mom was born and raised, and also after Mom and Dad got married they lived there and Dad worked for Grandpa. Mike and Nean lived there also till they moved to town around the time Mom was pregnant with me. I know Dad started working for the school the day after I was born.

Getting back to going to Uncle George's, they had a little girl that was very close to my age. I won't go into the fact that she was cute too. She was always thinner than me and had long black curls and Mike always made such a fuss over her that I grew to dislike her. Living on the farm, she had a pony and everything else she wanted, at least that's how it seemed to me. In time she had a brother and two sisters, and we had a lot of good times together as we got older.

Well, enough about her, the farm was about six miles south of Spalding. It was the same land my Great Grandpa John

Patrick "JP" Noonan settled when he came to the new country. He built a sod house to live in while he got the farm going. Later he built the house that is there now, 2016, falling down. He also built all the out buildings and a huge barn that is also gone. Three generations of Noonans farmed and raised cattle on this land. I drive by there whenever I'm over that way, just to stop and remember what fun we had when Grandpa lived there.

This is where my grandpa was born and raised and also my mother. My brother and sister were born here and raised till they were nine and ten years old also. My Grandpa Mike passed away December 2, 1949, and my Grandma Dolly had passed away May 8, 1924, when my mom was just twelve years old. So when Grandpa passed away all Mom had left was her brother, George, and two half-sisters.

Naomi & George on Logan...in front of the barn thier Grandpa (J.P. Noonan built)....

This Olds Home in Loo Valley as I fuilts it

This is the house Naomi Noonan was born & raised in......

Dad, holding me on the horse,
Darlene, Eleanor (Georges daughter), & Jeannine..
on the horse......

Mike

Mom

George
Mom's
Brother

November 1, 1942

CHAPTER 9

The Old Country School

There was a country school about half a mile east of Grandpa's. JP Noonan, along with others that had children, built this school, and JP taught there till they could find a teacher. JP's kids would have attended which would have been my grandpa and his siblings and then Grandpa's kids because he was the one who took over the farm from his dad, JP Noonan. Since Mom and Dad lived there when Mike and Jeannine started school, they too had the honor of attending the school their great-grandpa had helped build and taught at.

It broke my heart to see it falling down. Each time we would drive by it was in worse shape. Then one time the trees had gotten so thick I couldn't see it from that road, so I turned and as I passed it on the south road I was shocked to see it had been restored and made into a hunting lodge.

Thanks to Luke Rankin, the owner of the land, for saving some of the past. His family also had several generations attend that school. Luke told us that his dad didn't want it torn down so Luke took it upon himself to restore it to something that would be useful, so he turned it into a hunting lodge. He built an addiction on to the original building using a lot of farm wood that he was able to get from the Noonan farm and others, I assume. I hope I get to go stay in it overnight before I kick the bucket (in case you don't know what that means, it means pass away). Luke, if you're reading this book, I want to thank you for all you have done to save the old school.

This is the Leo Valley School...

Leo Valley School

John Patrick Noonan

Father of Michael Edward Noonan

CHAPTER 10

Going to Uncle John's

Getting back to the past, on Sundays we also went to Uncle John and Aunt Jessie's. This was my grandpa's brother. They lived on a farm farther south, almost to Wolbach. Talk about hills on that farm. Us kids thought they were mountains. Uncle John had thirteen children. That's a big family, but they all got along well and each of them had their work to do and everything always went smoothly.

One time when we were there they were raising sheep. Anyway, I remember going in and asking Aunt Jessie for a sack. I went out and picked up a whole bag of those little brown things that were all over their yard. I was sure it was chocolate candy. When the bag was full I went running into the house to show Aunt Jessie my bag of candy. I am so lucky I hadn't eaten any yet as it turned out it was really sheep poop. Everyone got quite a laugh out of that! Aunt Jessie traded me my bag of poop for a bag of goodies from her kitchen.

CHAPTER 11

My Birthdays

My birthdays were always special. Mom would make me an angel food cake and put fluffy white frosting on it with maraschino cherries all over it. Even though Don's birthday was a day ahead of mine, we would each get our own cake. Also almost every year I would have a birthday party.

My folks didn't have much money, so they were good at making due. For instance for birthdays and Christmas, Dad made me nice things out of wood. Some of the things he made me were a team of horses, a farm wagon, a doll cradle, table and chairs, a mower, an ironing board, a sled for riding in snow, and he made me a chest of drawers and dresser to keep my clothes in. Most everything he made me I still have. Daddy loved working with wood. I guess that's where I get it. He didn't have any nice tools like we have today, but he could make whatever he wanted.

5 years—1946

CHAPTER 12

Fishing with Daddy

Daddy also loved to fish, and he spent a lot of time fishing in the Cedar River that runs on the south side of Spalding. He kept us fed with his catches and we all loved fish. As soon as I was old enough, I'd go fishing with Dad. My first pole was a cane pole Dad bought at the hardware store. It was really long or at least it looked that way to me. He started me off fishing for carp. We didn't eat them but they were easier to catch. He had so much patience, he would untangle my line time after time and never get upset.

I can still see my dad digging for worms or sometimes he'd make his bait from cornmeal and cotton. At this time, the city sewer dumped into the river and we'd go there to catch carp. We would always throw them back, for who would want to eat them after what they had been eating? I can still hear Dad saying "Pull, Pug, pull" as the bobber would go underwater. I'd catch the fish, and he'd take it off the hook and throw it back, bait the hook, and we'd do it all again. This would continue until I'd get tired. By the way, Pug was the nickname Dad gave me and that's what he called me till he passed away.

When I got older I would go with him at night and fish for catfish. When we'd get to the river, it would still be light and I'd be fishing twenty feet or so away from him. The darker it got, the closer I'd get to him till finally I'd be sitting on his lap.

There are many strange sounds at the river after dark, and I learned what every one of them was because as soon as I'd hear a new sound I'd say, "What's that, Dad?" and he would tell me what was making the noise. Sometimes we'd catch fish and sometimes we wouldn't but it was a lot of fun.

Dad went fishing alone a lot of the time. I remember when he got his hip waders. Mom would worry herself to death till he got home because he'd walk down the river (in the water) fishing and he didn't even know how to swim. Of course, the river isn't too deep but there are some pretty deep holes. I think Dad knew where they all were because he had been fishing there for so long.

One night when he got home from fishing there were a bunch of ladies having lunch after their church meeting, which was at our house that night. The first thing said was "Did you catch anything?" Dad reached into his fishing bag, and with a big grin on his face, he pulled out this huge fish head. As he continued to pull it out, his grin turned into a dumbfounded look, for all he had to show them was a head and the bones. The ladies cracked up laughing and Dad's face turned bright red. It seemed a coon or something had a feast on Dad's fish while he was down the river a ways trying to catch another one. Well, he never did live that one down.

I remember one summer the town had a fishing contest for the kids. I wanted to go so badly, but Mom was sick and I needed to stay with her. I was sure wishing I could go, and then Dad came home from work and took me down. It was about over when we got there, but I threw in and within a few minutes I hooked a good one. I no more than got him out of the water when the whistle blew and the contest was over. Lo and behold, I had the biggest fish caught and took first place. Well, they hadn't figured a girl would win as I was supposed to get an overnight fishing trip to Lake Ericson with a bunch of guys. They worked it out so a boy could do that and I got a new rod and reel and a lot of fishing stuff. Dad taught me well.

Lots of times on Sunday afternoons the whole family would go to the river, Mom would bring a picnic lunch, and Dad would help us kids fish. By now I was getting pretty good at fishing, but Don was just learning. This one time, he actually caught a little fish. Mom and Dad kept telling him to throw it back in the river, but he wanted to keep it. Finally they gave up and after a while they noticed he wasn't carrying it around anymore, so they assumed he had threw it back. Well, a few days later, we all noticed a weird smell up in the boys' room. For the life of us, no one could figure out where it was coming from. To Mom's surprise, when she did the laundry that week, lo and behold, the fish was in the pocket of Don's pants. Everyone had a good laugh over that.

Dad and one of his big catfish he caught out of the Cedar River. Taken 1950's.

This would have been taken while we were getting new oak floors put in, notice the new flooring on the porch.

Having a picnic summer of 1946,
Mike, Me, Don, Dad & Mom,
Nean is taking the picture.

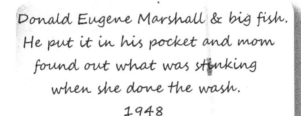

Donald Eugene Marshall & big fish.
He put it in his pocket and mom
found out what was stinking
when she done the wash.
1948

CHAPTER 13

Doing the Laundry Back Then

I mentioned a laundry room earlier. Well, laundry was a lot different then than it is today. We did our own once a week, usually on Monday if the weather would allow. Mom took in laundry to help pay bills, so sometimes she would be washing almost every day.

Back then we only had cold running water, so Mom would heat the water for the washing machine on the cook stove in a boiler, which was the biggest pot she had. While it was heating we would fill the two rinse tubs with cold water. The soak tub was filled with cold and enough hot to make it lukewarm. Also while we were waiting for water to heat we would sort clothes into piles, lights, medium, darks, underwear, towels, and so on. The dirty work clothes were last.

Things that needed soaking went in the soak tub while a load that didn't was being washed in the machine. When they had washed long enough, and Mom decided that, they would go through the wringer into the first rinse tub and then through the wringer into the second rinse tub and then through the wringer into a basket to be hung out on the line. Then the stuff in the soak tub would go into the washer and another into the soak tub, and this would go on until everything was on the line drying. Then washer and tubs had to be drained and cleaned so it was ready for the next washday. Also we had to take wet rags and wipe clean all of the clotheslines before we could hang clean clothes on them.

Dad had set poles in the ground and put up a lot of wire lines for Mom to hang clothes. He had one that went clear across the north end of the yard, two that went across the east side, and two shorter ones that were across the front yard. Most of the time we had these full and were waiting for some to dry so we could get the rest of them hung up to dry.

All the streets were gravel, so we tried to wash on a day when the wind was in the north or east. That way we didn't have to deal with all that dust. The birds we couldn't control, so if they pooped on something we just had to wash it over.

Back then everyone burned their garbage. Most of the people would check to make sure no one had clothes on the line before they started a fire. However, if one of the neighborhood ladies got upset with someone they would start a fire so it would blow smoke on their clothes, just for spite. I saw and heard a few neighbor ladies fighting over this. Anyway, it was a full day's work to wash the clothes, hang them out, bring them in, fold them up, and put them away.

Now washday in the winter was a whole different story. The washroom wasn't heated, and we still had to hang everything out. Sometimes the clothes would freeze before we could get them on the line. After they hung on the line for so long we would go pry them off and bring them in the house. It was no easy job getting frozen sheets and long underwear through a door. To finish drying we'd hang them on racks and set them over the floor furnace.

I asked Mom why we had to hang them outside in the first place and her answer was "so they smell good." It made no sense to me then and it still doesn't.

CHAPTER 14

Learning to Iron

A nother thing we did back then was iron. Mom would make starch, and the things that needed starched were starched before they were hung out. When we brought the dry clothes in, we would make a pile of starched things, sprinkle water on them, roll them up, and pack them in a basket so they would be damp all over when we went to iron them the next day. Sometimes we'd have as much as two bushel baskets full of ironing.

Mom taught me to iron by letting me iron the hankies and then I graduated on up to where I was going out to people's houses and ironing for them when I was in seventh or eighth grade. She taught me well. Back then perma press would have been great.

It's hard for me to figure out why anyone would want to buy clothes you have to iron. It's 2016, and you see people wearing these all cotton clothes and they are all wrinkled and look like heck. I don't think hardly anyone has an iron or ironing board anymore, and if they do they probably don't know how to use it. I'm just glad I know how but I only have to iron if I choose to.

CHAPTER 15

Mom's Sewing Machine

Another one of my fondest memories is about Mom's sewing machine. It was an old Singer Treadle machine. Mom did mending, but she didn't make a lot of stuff. The only thing I remember her making was a sundress for me with heart pockets. I was so proud of it I had to run to the neighbors to show it off. I always wanted to sew. I'd stand and watch as Mom did the mending and I kept asking her to teach me how to do it. It was always the same answer: "You're too young, or you'll sew your fingers."

I learned how to operate the machine just by watching. Mom would go downtown shopping about once a week and she always took me with her. Well, one day I told her I'd rather stay home and read, and she thought that was strange but she let me stay home. Now I knew about how long she'd be gone so I went to the rag box and started sewing. Everything went really well, but I had to get rid of the evidence before she got back. I always stayed home after that and had a ball making stuff for my doll, and then one day it happened! I sewed my finger, and when she got home I was sewed to the machine crying. She got my finger out and fixed it up and then said, "Well, if you're going to sew I'd better show you how." After that I never had to sneak around to sew, and because of that I made most of my clothes, and after I got married and had kids I made all their clothes including their underwear. Now I make quilts. I just can't get sewing out of my blood.

While I'm talking about sewing, I'll tell you about how a lot of ladies got new dresses. Take my Mom for instance. When she needed a new dress, she would go to the IGA Grocery Store—they had much more than food in this store—and buy a pattern, fabric, and thread, and then take it to the lady in town that did sewing. Sometimes Mom would order her pattern from an ad in the newspaper or the *Cappers Weekly*, which was a paper that came once a week. The lady that does sewing would fit the pattern to her, and in a few days Mom would have to go back for a fitting. When the lady had it fitted just perfectly, you would have to stand with the dress on while she pinned up the hem. In a few days the dress would be done. Mom would go get it and also the scraps that were leftover. That's where I got the scraps to make my doll clothes. I remember Mom taking me there to have dresses made. I don't know what it cost, but it was a lot cheaper than driving clear to Grand Island to buy one and then having to get it altered to fit when you got home.

This may be a good time to tell you about getting your hair fixed back then. We had maybe two beauty operators in town, and they would shampoo, curl, and cut your hair about like they do today, but getting a permanent was a whole different deal. I got my first one at four or five years old, and needless to say I didn't like it. What she would do was wash your hair and then roll it up in rollers—that was bad enough—and then she would sit you on a tall stool, and that's because I was so little. The ladies had a nice chair to sit on. Well, then came the very worst. She had this big thing that looked like one of those hair dryers you would sit under to dry your hair, but it had a lot of things hanging out of it. She would put one of these on each roller, and this took some time. That's why she always made sure you went potty before she started because once she hooked you up, you were there till you got cooked enough, and it seemed like that took an hour. I really thought she was going to electrocute me. Anyway, she'd turn it on and the rollers would all get hot, and sometimes it would burn your scalp. It was kind of like she baked curls into my hair. Well, when she finally got me out of there and got finished I looked really cute and the curls lasted for a long time. This was when I wished I had natural curly hair. By the way, you can be real thankful they don't have those things anymore!

CHAPTER 16

Getting a Phone

The telephone is something else we didn't have when I was little. I don't remember what year it was, but I remember getting our first phone. Back then they had party lines, and this meant you could have two, three, or four neighbors on your line, depending on how much you wanted to pay for your service. When the phone rang, you could tell if it was for you by the way it rang. A short, a long, two shorts and a long, and so on. When you answered, you could hear everyone else pick up their phones and listen. The phone was nice, but you really had to watch what you were saying on it.

Our phones were a lot different back then. They were hooked to the wall so you couldn't carry it around to wherever you'd go. Also the phones did one thing, put you in touch with another person. You had to talk to them as you couldn't write messages on the phone. Also if you weren't home, they just had to try later, and when someone came to visit, they visited with you and they had no phone to keep interrupting your visit. Guess what? We all got along fine without having to know everyone's business, and also we were able to get more exercise and people weren't so overweight. It was great growing up back then.

Don was painted up for a school play...Notice the Phone behind them.

CHAPTER 17

Heating the House

When I was telling you about the laundry, I mentioned the floor furnace. In the basement we had a big wood and coal burning furnace. Every fall the folks would buy a big load of coal to heat the house through the winter. The big truck would come and the guys would shovel the coal into the coal shoot which sent it down to the basement.

In the winter Dad would have to go down to the basement several times a day to keep a good fire going. The heat went straight up and came out the grate between the dining room and living room. It also went up the stairway; however, they kept some blankets hung up there so there was just enough heat that went up to keep the bathroom from freezing up.

I remember when Mom would wash my hair in the winter, she would lay me across two chairs with my head over the floor grate to dry my hair. The bedrooms were so cold, my sister and I would stand over the furnace and let our night gowns fill way up with heat, and then we'd run up and jump in bed and cuddle up trying to stay warm till we'd go to sleep.

Now you probably won't believe this, but when it would snow and blow from the north we would have a big snowdrift under the windows. After we ran downstairs and got dressed and warmed up, we would go back up and shovel the snow and put it in the bathtub so it would melt and run away. Dad always covered the windows with oilcloth (something like plastic today, only stronger). Somehow the snow would still find its way in.

CHAPTER 18

The Winter of '48 and '49

Speaking of snow, there was one advantage to living on a hill, you always had a hill to sleigh ride down. The winter of '48 and '49 was the worst winter ever, and you can read about it in history books. I lived through it, so I'll tell you what it was like for a seven- or eight-year-old. I remember people talking about how some were snowed in so badly that planes had to drop them off food. We were lucky to be living in town where we could get to the store; however, the stores ran short because they weren't getting anything in either. We were lucky because Mom canned plenty of food so we didn't go hungry.

I remember the snow was over the clothesline posts, but Dad found the clotheslines and dug them out for Mom. Also when they shoveled the sidewalks it was like walking through a tunnel, the sides were even over Dad's head. When it warmed up some, Don and I got to go out to play, finally. We took tin cans and stuck them in the walls of the tunnel, then we'd dump the snow out and use these little snow logs to build forts. We also built a lot of snowmen.

I think that the snow being so deep helped heat the house because the cold wind couldn't blow in the windows or in around the foundation. It was like having insulation all around your house. With the wind blowing as hard as it did the snow was packed so hard that you could walk on it and never sink in. Cars even drove over the big drifts as you couldn't tell where the roads or the light poles were.

It would be so nice to get snow like we got back then; however, we don't care to have that much all at once, ever again. Back then we'd get snow as early as October or November for sure. If we got ice, it would still be there come spring. There was always enough snow that we could go sleigh riding any time we wanted.

Look—I'm a Snowman! Winter 1945

Daddy & Daelene with sled he made her. Dec. 1944

CHAPTER 19

The Year Spring Couldn't Come Fast Enough

Spring was a busy time, Mom would be busy spring house cleaning and Dad would be busy planting his garden. My Mom was "Mrs. Clean" and God bless her for that. She taught me how to keep a clean house.

Every spring and fall the whole house would get cleaned, and everything but the wallpaper got washed, because back then it wasn't washable. We'd dust the walls and ceiling and wash the woodwork and windows, polish the furniture, scrub and wax the floors, and wash and iron the curtains. It was a lot of work, but it was worth it as we always had a spotless home.

CHAPTER 20

Dad's Garden

Now back to Dad. He always had a big garden. He always planted potatoes on Good Friday. Good Friday is the Friday before Easter Sunday. Everything else got planted once the danger of frost has passed. Dad used to say by May 15 the danger of frost should be over. He would raise potatoes, corn, tomatoes, carrots, onions, peas, beans, dill, peppers, and cucumbers.

In late summer and early fall, Mom would can jar after jar of vegetables as they had to last till the garden started bearing next year. Dad would buy her peaches, pears, and apricots as they became available, and she would can them up so we had fruit for the following year. We'd also go pick wild plums, chokecherries, elderberries, and sand cherries, and then Mom would make jellies from them. We also kept potatoes, carrots, and onions in the basement, and they would last most of the winter.

For several years, Dad had a huge strawberry bed in his garden and they were everbearing. I loved strawberries. As a matter of fact, when I was born I had a red spot on each shoulder that looked like strawberries, and in time they faded away. It seemed Mom had craved strawberries when she was carrying me.

Well, back to Dad's strawberries. Every day we would all have to help pick strawberries. Dad sold a lot of them and Mom made jam and jelly out of them also. Needless to say, we were all happy when he plowed up the strawberries and we didn't have to pick them anymore.

Back then they didn't have tillers, so in the spring Dad would have this guy with a horse come and plow his garden patch. It was too much garden for Dad to spade up by hand. One year the horse's leg went through what was an old well or cesspool. The horse didn't get hurt and Dad filled up the hole so us kids wouldn't fall into it.

CHAPTER 21

Playing in the Summer

In the summer when it would rain, all the water from up the hill would run through our yard, right down along the wraparound porch. With this big porch having a roof on it, we could play on it even if it was raining. One of Don's and my favorite things to do was go fishing in that river that was running right by our house. We would get sticks and tie a string to them, then tie a safety pin to the end and we would fish as long as the river kept running. Mom loved this game as it kept us out of her hair for a long time. Of course, we never caught anything.

Then when it was hot and dry, the ground would crack and look like a puzzle. We would pick out pieces of the puzzle and make roads to push our little toy cars around. Back then we had to use our imaginations as we didn't have all the fancy toys that kids have today, so we had to learn how to make up games and things to do.

For instance, the ditch on the west side of our yard, between the street and sidewalk, was where we played a lot. We would dig roads, for our little cars and trucks, into the bank, and also we'd dig garages to park them in. Sounds dumb now but we sure had a lot of fun back then doing it.

Also we liked to play ball. You just had to be careful, 'cause if you missed catching it or hitting it, you would have to chase it down the street a block before you could continue playing. We tried to train our dog Tinker to go get it for us, but he soon tired of that game. When Dad got home from work he would sometimes play with us. I have no idea where he got all his energy.

Another thing we did in the summer was hang blankets over the clothesline and make a tent, and then we could play like it was our fort or whatever we wanted it to be that day. Sometimes Mom would bring us out lunch and a cold drink. That was fun!

Roller-skating is another summer fun thing to do, and I was super good at it. Boy, I'd have been in seventh heaven with a pair of shoe skates. My skates hooked on the sole of my shoes and strapped on around my ankles. The worst part of skating was keeping your skates on. You could start skating at our house and go two or three blocks. That was the fun part, and then you had to skate uphill all the way home.

One summer Mom had sent me up to the neighbors for some reason, and on my way home, on the same sidewalk I skated on, I was running and lo and behold as I looked down there was a big snake coiled up where my foot was about to land. I don't know how I did it but since I was going too fast to stop I must have jumped right over it. Then I run twice as fast so I could get Dad and he'd get rid of it. Well, by the time we got back there the snake was gone. I guess I must have scared him as badly as he scared me, because we never saw that snake again. To be quite truthful I never did walk or skate on that part of that sidewalk again. If I needed to go that way I would walk in the street.

Another thing we always had fun doing was flying kites. Dad would cut us some thin strips of wood and then help us tie them together to look like a cross. Then we would find some brown paper that had been wrapped around something from the store or leftover wrapping paper from a birthday or Christmas. Dad would then help us get the paper glued on, and once this was done, we got in the rag box and tore strips of fabric about an inch or two wide. Once we got the tail tied on and a ball of string attached, off we went. The best place in town was just up the hill north of our house. The wind was good up there and there were no light wires or trees to get into. One of us would have the ball of string and we'd take off running and letting out string while the other would hold the kite as high as we could and we would run until a gust of wind would take it away. What fun it was to watch it go higher and higher. We took turns doing this, and when we heard Mom calling us for supper we'd have to bring it in while wrapping the string up so it would be ready for the next day the wind was blowing.

One summer Dad took some rope and an old water pipe and made me a trapeze. Betty and I had a lot of fun on it. I did pretty well, but Betty was much better. She could put her hands on the ground and bring her legs down and land on her feet. When I tried it I'd land on my face every time.

We spent a lot of time playing on the trapeze.

My friend, Irene Shamp, & me having fun with our homemade tent. Notice the old push mower (no motor). 1951

CHAPTER 22

Greeley County Fair

The county fair was always in the middle of August. Greeley was the county seat but Spalding had the fair. It lasted three days, and everyone would take their best garden stuff, sewing, handiwork, canned stuff, baked goods, you name it, and they took it to be judged. It would all be displayed in the school basement, and winners would be given money along with ribbons.

The livestock was housed in buildings at the fairgrounds just a couple of blocks south of the school. There you could find cattle, pigs, goats, sheep, chickens, ducks, rabbits, and about anything else that had two or four legs. They were all judged also.

There was always a parade, and Mom and Nean always dressed Don and me up so we could be in it. I don't know if we ever won anything, but we got a bunch of ride tickets for being in the parade.

Every night there would be a show in front of the grandstand. It was always free. That's why they called it the Greeley

County Free Fair. The best part of the fair was the rides. Mom would do washing for a lot of the people that worked for the fair, and most of the time they would give Mom a bunch of ride tickets in addition to the cost of their laundry. It worked out well because the folks didn't have much money to buy them.

The county fair was the biggest event that went on at Spalding. Everyone would come. The old folks would sit around and visit after they had seen everything, and kids would just have fun riding the rides and if they were lucky enough to have a little change in their pocket they could play some of the games and win some little thing. That little thing today, if it's in good shape, would probably be worth more than one would spend all three nights at the fair back then.

Early in the morning after it was over, the carnival people were all gone and people were picking up the stuff they had on exhibition. You could go to the fairgrounds and pick up empty pop bottles and look under the grandstand for things people may have dropped, like money. Back then you could sell pop bottles for five cents each, and it was a good way for us kids to make some money.

CHAPTER 23

About the School

We lived one block north of the public school where Daddy worked. Guess what? It was all downhill going but it was all uphill coming home.

The school was a large brick building which sat on a whole city block. I want you to think about how many steps my dad had to climb every day. You had to go up a flight of steps to get to the front door, and then there was a flight going up to the first floor and another going up to the second floor and another short flight going up to the superintendent's office.

Now from the front door you'd go down one flight to the locker rooms and Dad's workroom, another flight down to the furnace room and stage and yet another one down to the gym. I wouldn't even venture a guess as to how many stairs he would do in just one day. Maybe that's what kept him so healthy and ambitious.

On the first floor was five large rooms and the boys' and girls' restrooms. One of the large rooms was the kitchen and dining room, one was the home ec room, and the other three were classrooms for kindergarten through eighth grades.

The second floor was the high school, and it had a large assembly room and five classrooms plus the restrooms. There was another short flight of stairs going up to the superintendent's office, and from here you could see everything that was going on. It was also the room you never wanted to get sent to by your teacher.

As you got to the top of the stairs on the second floor there was a big hallway, and in the center of it, just before you go into the assembly room, there was a round porcelain water fountain. This was used to jump over as long as no teachers were present. Along the south wall was a heat register where my dad would be standing waiting to ring the morning or noon bell. There was a bell rope coming down from the ceiling. If I close my eyes, I can still see Dad pulling the rope and ringing the bell.

This is the Giant Stride

CHAPTER 24

How Did One Man Do It All?

D ad's job included a lot of other things he had to do. For instance he had to sweep every room, hall, and steps on the first and second floors every day there was school. Plus he cleaned every bathroom and water fountain daily.

In the winter the whole school was heated with a coal burning furnace, which meant the stoker had to be kept full of coal, and the hot steam would travel through the pipes to each register in the building in order to keep every part of the building warm. Of course, it was Dad's job to keep the registers running properly and the stoker full of coal.

In the winter Dad would have to make one or two trips down to the school every night to fill the stoker. Going down was bad enough but coming home was awful. He not only was going uphill but had the north wind and snow blowing in his face. I remember sometimes he would be shivering and shaking so badly when he got home that we would have him sit over the floor furnace and wrap him up in blankets to get him warmed up.

In the summer it was just the opposite. He had to mow the whole block where the school was with an old push mower. That's a mower without an engine, and many a time he got overheated doing that. Also in the summer he would repaint most of the schoolrooms and also refinish the gym floor.

When I got older I would help Dad sweep floors sometimes. I sure wish now that I'd have helped him more. I believe that Don helped Dad a lot as he got older. When I graduated in 1959, Dad was sixty-six years old, and when Don graduated in 1963, Dad would have been seventy years old. How a man of that age could do what he did is beyond me. Finally in the mid-'60s Dad retired.

Here is something you won't believe, in 1959 when I graduated, Dad got paid only $200 a month. Maybe a little more, all I know is Dad and Mom worked their butts off to make a go of it. The thing of it is we didn't know we were poor. We always had something to eat and clothes on our backs even though they were patched. We were all happy and enjoyed living. I think the people today are really missing out on so very much. They are so busy making money so they can own a big house, a new car, expensive clothes, shoes, and purses, that they have no time to walk barefoot in the grass, go fishing on a hot day and dangle your feet in the cool water, break a watermelon in pieces and eat it by hand while it drips all over you, play ball with your kids, just for fun. I could go on and on as there are many things you can do without money. I'm just glad I grew up back then when we were allowed to be kids.

An Old Familiar Sight

Roy Marshall - Janitor

CHAPTER 25

Sharing My School Memories

I went to kindergarten at age five. Mrs. Zahm was my teacher. She had already taught Mike and Jeannine in their lower grades, and she would also be Don's teacher when he started school.

Not bragging but that first year was so easy for me that the teacher and my folks agreed that I should skip first grade and go right into second. This proved to be a big mistake because from then on, school was hard for me. I always passed and got average grades, but I think it would have been a lot easier for me if I would have gone to first grade.

I don't remember what grade I was in when this happened. When school started that year, the teacher had us all filling out papers. They had all kinds of questions, one of them being, "What's your nationality?" Well, all I knew about that was that Dad always said I was a Blue-Bellied Yankee, so that's what I put down. The teacher had to tell Dad about it, and I guess they really had a good laugh.

At recess we had swings, teeter-totters, and the giant strides to play on. I'm sure you don't know what a giant stride is, so I'll try to explain it to you. It was a tall pole with several chains hanging from its top. The chains had handles you could hold on to, and then you would run around it as fast as you could, and when it got going fast enough all you had to do was hang from the chain and swing around it till it went too slow, and then you'd have to run again. It would hold about six kids at a time.

Today you will not find a giant stride anywhere as they would be a hazard to kids. If someone let loose of one it could fly around and hit someone; however, back then we had enough sense to duck. It seems all the fun stuff are off-limits to kids today. All they have is plastic stuff and handheld phones.

As we got older we would play softball at recess and lunch break. I didn't eat at school very often since we only lived a block away and Mom was home all the time and always had something fixed for us. When I'd get back to school I'd get put on one team or the other, and we'd play till the bell rang, letting us know it was time to go back in.

CHAPTER 26

My First Boyfriend

y best memory about second grade was Donnie Sweat. I thought he was a hunk! Blond hair, blue eyes, and just really cute. I guess he liked me too as one day when he walked by my desk he gave me a note, and it said, "Come back to the book room." The book room was a long narrow room at the back of the classroom with double doors. It was used to store books and school supplies.

Well of course, I went back there and we both pretended to be looking for books, but as soon as we got past the doors and were out of sight of the teacher, he kissed me, and that was my first boy kiss and I'll always remember it. I was madly in love with him all through grade school, but then every other girl in school was too.

When we were going into ninth grade, his parents moved to Washington State, and that was the last I ever saw or heard from him, until I went back to our old school to celebrate my fiftieth alumni. Guess who was there? Donnie Sweat.

Well, after a big hug we had a nice visit. I was remembering back when he still lived here I used to pray that I'd be his wife someday. Well, as I watched him as the night went on I was thanking God for unanswered prayers. If we had gotten married I wouldn't have the four children I have and the wonderful husband. It just goes to prove "God knows what he's doing."

CHAPTER 27

School Programs

In grade school we always had a Christmas program, and most of it was singing. I remember one year our class was singing "Silver Bells," I was standing by Donnie Sweat and we were both ringing bells. Funny what a person remembers.

Many times they would have all the kids standing on bleachers to form a Christmas tree. The lights would be turned way down so all you could see was each of us holding a candle as we sang Christmas songs. Someone always got to be the star at the top of the tree. I wanted so much to be the star, but that never happened.

In high school we did a big three-act play once or twice a year. I always got a leading part. I think it was because my voice carried well and I was also good at acting. This may have been another calling I missed. Ha! Ha!

CHAPTER 28

My Best Friend Ever

Well, let's go back again. I never told you about my best friend, Betty Ann Buhrman. Her and her mom and dad moved into the big two-story house kitty-corner (that would mean southwest in this case) to us. I'm not sure what year it was, but I was pretty young. Betty's and my birthdays are the same day and we are the same age. I had a little brother, Don, and she had a little sister, Patricia. Her dad owned the Buhrman Implement in town, and they sold and worked on the red tractors and farm machinery. Betty's mom was a tall slim lady that always looked like she just stepped out of a model mag. Her mom, like mine, stayed home and took care of the house and kids. They moved here from California and they were really nice people.

Betty and her family were Catholic, so they went to the Catholic church. My family was Presbyterian, and we attended that church. Betty went to the Catholic school and I went to the public school. Of course, they seemed to be going to church all the time, but we just went on Sunday. Betty's mom told about one morning she was getting Betty up to go to early mass when Betty asked her, "Why do I have to go to church so much, Darlene says she's going to heaven and she only has to go to church on Sunday." Everyone got a big kick out of that one.

We played at each other's houses most every day. We had to ask permission, and then our moms would call each other and see if it was OK with them. We could stay for an hour, maybe less or maybe more depending on the time of day it was. I had lots of other friends back then, but they seemed to move away after time, but Betty was always there.

I remember back when we were twelve or thirteen years old Betty came up to my room and pulled out cigarettes. I don't know where she got them. She wanted us to smoke them. I was always the chicken and didn't want to, but she talked me into smoking with her. There we were both puffing on our cigarettes, and all was going well until we heard Mom coming upstairs. Stupid us, we laid both cigarettes on the ashtray and slid it under my dresser. Mom walked into my room and said, "I smell smoke." We assured her we weren't smoking, but the smoke was rolling out from under my dresser. Needless to say, we weren't allowed to see each other for a while, not to mention the chewing out we both got, plus extra chores. Of course, Mom called her mom and we didn't ever try that again. By the way, I thought it tasted awful.

Betty wasn't afraid of anything, unlike me. She would catch mice and play with them. One day she came up before school and handed me a box. I opened it and nearly had a heart attack. She had caught a mouse and brought it up to me. I guess that's when she realized I really don't like mice, so she grabbed it, before I could faint, and got gone before my mom saw it.

One day Betty tried to get me to break her arm so she wouldn't have to do dishes, but of course, I chickened out.

Back then when we went to Grand Island, you could go to the Five and Dime store and buy a little turtle, which would be painted up really pretty. This was all the thing for a while back then. Well, we all had pet turtles. Betty was taking a bath one day when she decided to take her turtle in with her. She filled the tub up with hot water and dropped the turtle in, and she got in intending to play with him, but he had his legs and head pulled in and they wouldn't come out so Betty thought she had killed the turtle. After her bath she took the turtle—still with his legs and head pulled in—out and buried him in the garden before her mom found out what she had done. Well, her mom realized the turtle wasn't in his box and Betty had to tell her what happened. Her mom sent her back to the garden to dig up the turtle, and lo and behold the turtle was still alive.

I remember one Halloween when we wanted to do something exciting but we didn't want to hurt anyone's property, so we decided we'd string the lumber her dad had piled up behind their garage down the alley. We had a lot of fun trying to do it without getting caught. We thought we had gotten away with it, but the next morning her dad had us out there picking it all up and stacking it up where it had been. I really think he must have watched us and figured as long as we were doing it there we wouldn't be getting in trouble somewhere else.

Betty and I were best friends until we graduated from high school and moved away from Spalding. We were busy raising kids, dealing with men, and trying to make a living for our families. Now in the golden years, ha-ha, we have reconnected and try to see each other often.

Best Friends
Donnie-Me-Betty Buhrman

This is Betty & Me in our girlscout uniforms.
1951

CHAPTER 29

Our New Refrigerator

M y big brother, Mike, worked for Betty's dad at Buhrman Implement. They sold and serviced farm equipment, and they also sold cars and other stuff. I remember when Mike brought home a new refrigerator. It was an electric international brand. Now we could make our own ice cubes. Before the new fridge, we had an ice box. An ice box was a big fancy wood box with two doors. It was divided into two sections, one to hold the ice and one to hold the food you needed to keep cool. The ice would keep the food cool until it all melted, and then you would have to go to the ice man and get another big chunk of ice.

The ice man had a building with a big hole dug in the dirt floor, and here he would store his ice he had gotten in the winter, under a lot of straw. The ice would be cut into large blocks, and that's where we got our ice. The electric ice box was so much easier.

CHAPTER 30

Mom Trying Something New to Her

Nean worked at Coynes IGA Grocery Store. It was right across the street, south of where Mike worked. Back then you could go into the store and have them write down the cost of your purchase and on payday you would go in and pay up your bill. Back then people were honest and paid their bills.

To get back to the story, Mom would call the store and have Nean bring home this or that, whatever she needed. Well, all of a sudden Mom was calling every day and having Nean bring home a different brand of cigarettes for Dad, she'd say. Well, Dad was liking this because I'm pretty sure he usually bought them himself. He often wondered why they were opened and always one missing; however, he wasn't going to look a gift horse in the mouth. All at once it stopped and he later found out that Mom had been trying each brand, trying to find one she liked so she could smoke with Dad. Needless to say, she ran out of brands and didn't like any of them.

CHAPTER 31

Going to the Meat Market

O ne of the things I remember doing for Mom was going to the meat market. She would give me a dollar bill so I could get a dollar's worth of hamburger or homemade sausage for supper. Back then a dollar's worth of meat would feed a family of six, with enough leftover for Dad's lunch the next day.

Another thing I remember is almost every day about 4:30 or 5:00 p.m. Mom would call me in so I could peel potatoes for supper. I had to peel a lot, so we would have leftovers to fry for lunch the next day. I don't much like peeling potatoes, but after all that practice I'm pretty good at it.

CHAPTER 32

Christmas Back Then

Christmas was a special time and (unlike today) it took a long time to get here. Mom would always make her filled cookies way early and store them in the pantry till Christmas. The older they got, the better they were, and of course I'd sneak in and have one as often as I could. They were so good. Following Mom's tradition I bake up a lot of filled cookies for Christmas so I can give them away for the holidays.

Mom also made a lot of candy for the holidays like peanut brittle, fudge, and everyone's favorite Orleans candy. She tried to make divinity, but it just never worked and I don't have any luck with it either.

I can't remember Mom ever using a candy thermometer. She would have a bowl of cold water nearby and drop a few drops of candy in it and keep cooking until it made a soft or hard ball, whichever she needed, and everything always turned out perfect except for divinity.

At church we would start right after Thanksgiving, getting our parts and learning the songs for our Christmas program. I remember singing "Away in a Manger" all by myself when I was pretty little.

We would have our program on Christmas Eve, and after it was over, Santa would come and we'd all get a bag of candy and fruit. After church we would go home and I would toast bread for Mom so she could make the dressing for the turkey.

We really did have Charlie Brown Christmas trees back then. They had very few branches and if you know what Charlie Brown's tree looked like, ours was just like that and we were glad to have it. The branches could hardly hold up the few lights that we did have and some really pretty decorations.

I must tell you about the pink and blue glass bells that went on the tree every year since I was two years old. It was told that just before Christmas the year I turned two, Mom was in the grocery store getting her groceries and as she was walking out she saw that I had two pretty bell decorations, one in each hand. Well, she turned me around and made me give them back to the store owner and told him I was sorry for taking them. He spent some time trying to convince Mom that it was OK and he wanted me to have them. At any rate I didn't get to take them with me, but when Mom unpacked her groceries, here were the bells all wrapped up with my name on them. Mom broke down and let me hang them on the tree and the next time we went to the store she made sure I thanked the man. One bell came up missing when my boys were pretty young. I always think that they broke it and they probably thought I'd never notice one decoration missing. Of course I noticed, but they said they knew nothing about it. In the 1990s, my last bell got broken. My daughter and her husband had come up one weekend, we got the tree up and decorated, and then we went out for the evening. When we came home, here was the tree lying down on the floor with only one decoration broke, and yes, it was my last bell. Every time I see a bell decoration at Christmas I think of my pink and blue bells.

As the Christmas lights got more plentiful Dad and my sister, Nean, would put up blue lights on our house. Sometimes they would make the blue lights look like a cross. From main street, it looked like our house had a halo around it, and it was really pretty.

Daddy never liked Christmas too much because with the extra cost of coal to heat the house he just didn't have money to buy gifts. He made me a lot of very special things like a dresser and chest of drawers, a doll bed that rocks, a table and chairs, a mower, a sled, an ironing board, a hay rack and horses, just like Grandpa had on the farm. These are just some of the things he made me, and as you see I still remember them and I still have a lot of them. I really can't remember the things people bought me. Daddy made things for the others in the family too.

As kids, even though we didn't have a lot of money we always got a lot of gifts. I think Mom started putting away a little of her baking and laundry money so we could have a nice Christmas. Don and I each got a couple of toys and that's when we got most of our winter clothes. We thought we were in seventh heaven.

Nean always helped Santa out. One of the things I remember was my first all-rubber doll. I still have that doll, but the rubber is turning black and it is starting to rot. The other thing was my first bike, and actually it was my only bike. Nean and Dad were in this together, it was a used bike they got from someone, and they painted it blue. It was the best and fastest bike in town. It was a boy's bike but I didn't care. I could race the boys and beat them every time. I loved that bike. I still remember Nean standing in the living room with her big robe pulled way out trying to hide the bike as I peeked around the stairway that Christmas morning.

On Christmas morning Mom always had cinnamon rolls for breakfast. After we had opened our gifts and had breakfast, I'd have to go down to Betty's and see what she got and she'd come up and see what I got.

I'm sure glad that God gave us minds to record our memories. Just think how awful it would be if we couldn't remember all the wonderful things we've done and places we've been and people we've known. Also it's amazing how we can remember all the good stuff and the bad stuff just fades away.

This looks like a real Charley Brown Christmas. 1942 or 43 ?

This is my bike I got for Christmas. I wanted a bike so bad and I was sure I Would'nt get one because we could'nt aford it, but Dad & Nean found a used one & fixed it up like new. I thought it was wonderful!!! I rode it a lot & I could ride better than any boy. Life was Great!! I think it was 1952or53.

CHAPTER 33

About My Pets

I never told you about my pets.

At one time or another I have had rabbits, ducks, chickens, cats, turtles, and fish. The only one that I'll always remember is Tinker, my dog. Now Mom sure didn't believe in having animals in the house so they all lived outside except for the turtles and fish.

Now back to Tinker. He was just a ball of black and white fur when we got him. Mom did let him sleep inside in a box until he got used to being without his mommy. I remember we put a hot water bottle and stuffed toys in with him and also a clock that ticked. All this to make him think his mommy was there. I have always thought that the first few nights he slept with Mom but she'd never admitted to it. I don't know where we got the name Tinker, but anyway, he grew up to be my best friend. I told him all my troubles and he was always there for me to cry on.

I knew he didn't like baths, but in the summer he got a few anyway. He was raised on Purina Dog Chow. When my son

Kenny and I were living with my folks while Edward, my husband, was in the service, Kenny would get into the dog food on the porch. I would find him sitting there giving Tinker a piece and then having a piece for himself. I figured if it didn't hurt Tinker it wouldn't hurt Kenny. I guess it didn't as he grew up to be a fine young man. I don't know how old Tinker was when the folks had to have him put to rest, but all I know is that he was missed by the whole family.

CHAPTER 34

Riding the Train to Visit Uncle Bill and Aunt Mary

B ack when I was a child the big old steam engine train came to Spalding. We had a depot, and you could buy tickets and ride many places. That's what brought a lot of our freight to town. I remember you could hear the horn blowing at road crossings as it got nearer and nearer to town. It was so much fun to be there to watch as it stopped and then got going again.

Well anyway, when I was five or six years old, my folks decided to let me ride the train down to Fullerton where my Aunt Mary and Uncle Bill lived. They would be there to pick me up, and I would stay with them for maybe a week or so, and then they would put me back on the train and I would ride it back home.

I was so excited I couldn't wait for the day to come, but finally it did, but then I didn't think the train would ever get there, but it did. There I was going up the steps with my little suitcase. I felt like such a big girl, but as the train started to move I got a little scared and was about to cry when the conductor came and sat by me. Dad had already talked to him, and since I was the only passenger that day, he made sure I got to Uncle Bill's all safe and sound.

Uncle Bill was there to meet me, and I was so glad to see him. He took me back to his house where Aunt Mary was waiting for me. You see, at that time they had two boys which were teenagers and they were having trouble getting a little girl so they spoiled me to pieces. One day it was raining and it just wouldn't stop. I guess I was getting bored so Aunt Mary somehow got one of the boy's raincoats fixed so I could wear it, and somewhere she found overshoes that almost fit. She handed Uncle Bill an umbrella and we walked to the Five and Dime store, and Uncle Bill got me a coloring book and colors. That was so much fun. I think I stepped out of a boot a couple of times, but Uncle Bill would slip it back on me and we'd be off again, splashing in all the puddles.

By the way if you don't know what a Five and Dime store is, I'll try to explain it to you. It was kind of like our dollar stores today, but they were usually a lot bigger and they had better things in stock. You could get some nice things for just five or ten cents. Now it's a dollar and the things you buy are cheaply made. It seems like everything today is made to fall apart so you can throw it away and spend more money to replace it.

When it came time for me to go home, I got to ride the train again and the same nice conductor made sure I got home safely. I was really glad to see Mom and Dad, but I was going to miss Aunt Mary and Uncle Bill.

It was a great ride, and if it were still running I'd go ride it again; however, the train stopped coming to Spalding. I can't remember when, but there isn't a trace of it anymore. Such a shame.

This is me with Dad's brother & wife Uncle Bill & Aunt Mary Marshall. Taken fall of 1944.

CHAPTER 35

Staying with Aunt Mary and Uncle Lawrence

Uncle Bill was my dad's brother as was Uncle Lawrence. Well, as I got older maybe about seven or eight years, I remember staying in Grand Island with Aunt Mary and Uncle Lawrence. The folks took me down one weekend, and Uncle Lawrence brought me home the next. This was kind of my summer vacation. Uncle Lawrence worked for the railroad. I'm not sure what he did, but I know they only lived a block or two away from the tracks. It was really noisy there as the trains were always honking as they were coming and going somewhere. It was hard to get to sleep.

The one thing I remember doing while I was there was walking downtown with Aunt Mary. It was quite a ways, and sometimes I had a hard time keeping up. Aunt Mary was pretty spry for an older lady. It was fun looking at all the houses and seeing the kids play in their yards. There was one thing very strange to me. There was a man whose house we passed on the way downtown, and he had black skin. I had read in books about black people, but I had never seen a real one before. If he was outside when we walked by, Aunt Mary would always stop and talk to him for a while. He was such a nice and polite man. I kind of wished we had one, like him, at Spalding.

Well, we'd finally got downtown and Aunt Mary would do her shopping and we'd always stop at the Five and Dime store where she would let me buy something with my dime. We'd have a soda or ice cream and then head home. I would get to help her carry her purchases home.

There is one more thing I remember about being in Grand Island. They had built an underpass at the railroad tracks. They made a road that went under the trains. This made it nice because you didn't have to wait for trains to pass by. Well anyway, whenever Uncle Lawrence would drive under it with us kids in his car, he would honk his horn all the way through. We loved it. It kind of made an echo or something, but whatever it did, we'd never let him forget to honk.

Soon it was time for me to go home, so we would get up early and have a nice hour or two ride to Spalding where Mom would have dinner waiting for us. Life back then was so simple, and people liked spending time together. Now it seems like everyone would rather sit by themselves and play with their phones. Oh, my. I really feel sorry for all the stuff kids are missing out on today.

CHAPTER 36

Staying with Aunt Edie and Uncle Don

Another place I liked to stay was just outside Spalding a ways. This was a farmer Mike, my brother, worked for in the summer. We called them Aunt Edie and Uncle Don, and they were really good friends of my folks. Back then, TVs were just coming out and they had one. On one certain night there was a cowboy show that was on, so they would ask us out to watch it. Well, some nights you could see everything that was going on and then other nights all you could see was snow, but you could hear it so we were happy. We finally got a TV in the '50s. I think it was after Mike and Nean graduated and they were both working full-time jobs and living at home. It seemed they got it for us.

I got to go out and stay with Aunt Edie and Uncle Don once in a while, and it was so much fun. I got to go in the barn and watch them milk the cows. The barn cats would show up, and Uncle Don would give them a shot of milk right from the cow. After the milking was done, the milk would be taken to the separator shed. Aunt Edie would separate the milk from the cream. This was done by pouring the milk in a big stainless steel bowl and they would turn the handle, and milk would come out one place and cream another. The cream would then be poured into a steel can with a lid. This was called a cream can. Then they took some milk to the house to use, and I think the other was fed to the pigs and cats. That was not the end. Aunt Edie would have to take all the steel parts from the separator in and wash them so they would be ready for next time. They had to do all this twice a day along with all the other stuff farmers had to do. On Saturday night, all the farmers would bring their cream and eggs to town, sell them, and then they would get their groceries and spend the rest of the night visiting with other farmers and friends.

This is our folks good friends, Don & Edie Thompson. I use to got stay with them, on the farm, for a few days at a time. It was so much fun.

CHAPTER 37

Our First Vacation

My Grandpa Noonan passed away on December 2, 1949, and Mom was left a small inheritance which she used to buy a new 1950 Ford two-door. We had never had a new car before, so it was quite a big deal to us. That year we also took a trip up to South and North Dakota to see some of Dad's family that he hadn't seen for years.

I remember the day we finally were all in the car and Dad was driving away, he looked over at Mom and said, "Are you sure you don't want me to go back and get the kitchen sink, that's the only thing you didn't pack." We all got a laugh out of that. We had never gone on a trip before, and Mom didn't know exactly what to take so she took all she could get into the car. Now we were off.

This was the summer after Mike and Nean had graduated, so Mike was old enough to help Dad with the driving and Nean got the job of entertaining Don who was five years old, and I was eight years old. It's a good thing there were only six of us as we filled the car up real good.

I can remember staying at motels along the way. Nean told me that before Mom would take one, she'd have to look it over, make sure it was clean and would open up the beds and check for bed bugs.

We didn't eat in cafes very much as we would stop in towns and Mom would buy things we could fix and have picnics. The motels had kitchens, and Mom would fix us a nice meal in the evening. Other than that I don't remember much about the motels.

We did stop and have our evening meal at a cafe one night, and it was pretty fancy. They had a waiter with a towel hanging over one arm, and he took our order. Mom said we would all have the same thing, which I think was roast beef. Well, he brought us each a plate full of food, and then he would come around again with the roast beef and offer us more. He did that with everything that had been on our plates. What I really remember was when he asked Donnie if he'd like some more peas. Don looked up and in his big deep voice said, "No, sir, I already went pee." Everyone in the cafe heard it, and the whole place broke out in a laugh.

It seemed like everywhere we went, people thought that Mike and Nean were Don's and my parents and that Mom and Dad were our grandparents. Most of the time we just let them think that as it was easier than trying to make them believe it was the other way around.

When we got to the Black Hills we were all expecting to see a bear. Well, the first thing one of us spotted was a rabbit and then a squirrel. After some time we finally started see-ing signs saying "Stay in your cars" and "Don't feed the bears." That's when we started to see a lot of cars stopped along the road. Finally we spotted a bear and she had two babies with her. We sat there on the side of the road and waited, hoping she would come closer but she didn't, so Dad got out and went toward it trying to get her to come closer. She seemed to be ignoring Dad, until she had enough of it and started running at full speed toward him. Dad turned and ran as fast as he could, jumped in the car, and slammed the door shut. Mom calmly said, "I told you, you shouldn't get out." Anyway we got to see a bear close up.

We stopped at Mount Rushmore and saw the four heads carved in stone. It was nice, but I liked the gift shop better. I remember getting a small doll there. When we were riding and I got a bit bored, Nean showed me how to fold Kleenex to make doll clothes out of them, and that kept me busy for some time.

We also went to the Passion Play in South Dakota. It was a huge outdoor theater where live people portrayed the life of Christ from his birth to the cross. It was really something won-derful to watch. It's funny how things shrink as you get older. I had a chance to see it again when my children were small and we took them there. It was not nearly as big as it was when I was a child.

Not to change the subject, but a few years ago when all us Marshall kids were at Spalding for alumni, the lady that lived in our old house said she would let us go through it if we'd like.

We were all thrilled as none of us had seen it since the folks sold it. Well, they had made some changes but it was pretty much like we remembered it except we all noticed how small it had gotten. To this day I have no idea how Mom ever got so many people in that dining room to feed. I know people were not smaller back then. I guess it's how big you are when you're looking at something that leaves an impression on how big it is. Now back to the vacation.

Finally we got to Deadwood, South Dakota, where Aunt Annie lived. Her husband had a barbershop downtown and they lived on a big hill just south of Boot Hill Cemetery. We had a great time there, and we stayed with them for a few days and got to see most of the town and sightseeing places.

We also went on farther north to North Dakota and saw more of Dad's family. Since we were so close to Canada we drove on up there, crossed the border, drove around a little, and then left. At least we can say we had been to Canada.

Then the decision was made that we would drive through the Teton Mountains on the way back. Mom was not for this, but she was outvoted so away we went. Mike was driving and Mom was sitting by Dad. As we were going through the mountains, Mom had a hold of Dad's pants, and it seemed like it calmed her as she twisted a bit of them. When we stopped and got out, we all got a laugh as Dad had little picks of fabric all over his upper pant leg. Mom never did live that one down.

Soon our vacation was over, and it was a good time for all of us. I know we did other things, but these are the things that stuck in my mind. The thing I learned from this is to do things with your children that will make good memories for them in their old age.

This was Don & I standing on a rock overlooking a lake, In Yellowstone National Park, while we were on our family vacation in 1950.

CHAPTER 38

My First Year of High School

School started on the last Monday of August 1955. I was one of the first ones to get to school. Since this was my first year in high school, I was pretty nervous. I couldn't even eat breakfast. As soon as I got to school, I started looking for Judy O'niel. She was one of my best friends and a classmate. Instead I met Marie Carr, a junior, and we walked a couple of blocks to where Shirley and Bonnie Crosby, two more juniors, were staying and walked back to school with them. By this time the last school bell was ringing, so we went upstairs and joined the other kids.

In the freshman class there were nine of us. John Falls, Donnie Sweat, and Judy O'niel were the ones that graduated with me from eighth grade. The ones that came in from country schools were Jack and Carrol Hinze, Eugene Harnipp, Lonnie Clemets, and Rosrmarry Ecarad.

In the tenth grade, there were four boys, David Gillroy, Dennis McKay, Edward Bloom, and Gene Bittner.

The junior class had Shirley and Bonnie Crosby, Marie Carr, and Gary Climents.

The seniors were Lea Miller, Janice Harnipp, LaVonne Gilroy, Bob Porter, and Ronnie Gilroy. Later in the year Jack Soll joined them.

The teachers were Mr. Phillips, also the superintendent, Mrs. Dunning, and Mrs. Rhoads. Mr. Phillips taught me general science and lab. Also he was our coach for all our sports. Mrs. Rhoads taught math and English. Mrs. Dunning taught world geography and home economics.

The first day of school, we got our books and found out which rooms we went to for each class and who was teaching that class. We also had to register, which meant filling out a bunch of papers. After getting to meet all the kids and teachers, school was dismissed for the day.

My dad was the janitor and everything else. He fixed whatever needed fixed, he kept the school clean, and he set up the chairs and tables for everything that went on at school. He kept the whole block the school sat on mowed, and in the summer he would repaint the bathrooms, classrooms, and whatever needed painting. Also he would refinish the basketball floor. The year I started high school was his eighteenth year working for the school.

Since we only had a half day of school I went to work that afternoon at Mrs. McNad's. Her husband was the chiropractor at Spalding. I cleaned house for her, did her ironing, and whatever else she wanted done. I made thirty-five cents an hour, and that wasn't too bad back then. Mom called that day and told me that I was supposed to start work at Don's Cafe that night. I had applied for a job earlier. I liked working there as I got to see more people and learned how to be a good waitress. I was making thirty-five cents an hour, but I got more hours in than I did at my other jobs, and also I got tips. The tips were usually five or ten cents but they added up.

This brings to mind the time I had to be at work really early in the morning as it was hunting season. Back then there were a lot of birds to hunt and this brought to town a lot of guys from Omaha and other places. They would be in to eat at the cafe before the sun came up. One morning I went to the table to get their order and one of them asked if we had any cake. Me, thinking like sheet cake, said we might have one piece left from yesterday. They all started laughing and I didn't have a clue why, and finally the guy said he meant pancakes. Well, I felt pretty stupid but I apologized and took their orders. That morning they left me a ten-dollar tip. Wow! That was almost a week's wages.

Getting back to school, two weeks after school started we had an initiation. This was where the seniors welcomed the freshmen to high school. They had us wear funny things to school that day. I had to wear an old-fashioned swimsuit and cowboy boots. Half the swimsuit I borrowed from Helen Weber and the bloomers I got from Martha Kinnier and the boots from Frankie Glasinger. We all wore onions around our necks, and I had to wear a sign that read "Miss Onion Patch of

1955." They made us play leapfrog down the middle of main street, with eggs in our hands. We had to sing in the tavern, and Carol Hinze had to do the hula dance.

That night we were supposed to have a party, but because of severe storm warnings we had it the next night. At the party we got our faces painted and were made to pick up things while we were blindfolded and guess what it was. Like they piled grapes and told us they were eyeballs and made us eat worms which were really spaghetti, and also we all got a small electric shock. That was the worst. All in all, it was a lot of fun once we passed the torture part. So now we were officially high school students.

Something else I want to tell you about back then, we had a school bus for taking the sport teams to other towns to compete; however, as far as kids getting to school, the parents brought them and picked them up until they were old enough to drive. Now in the winter when the weather was bad, they would board kids with people in town, because the school stayed open and if you couldn't make it to school you had to make up all what you had missed. My folks always had one or two kids staying with them when bad weather was forecasted. I think their parents brought in meat, eggs, milk, and cream, and that's how they would pay for their child's keep if they didn't have the cash, which most of them were just like my folks, pinching every penny just to get by. It worked out well as those were the things the folks needed and the farmers had.

CHAPTER 39

Staying with a Friend

When I was in high school, I remember staying with one of my classmates for a few days one summer. Her name was Darlene too, and anyway, they lived on a farm between Spalding and Greeley. There are two things I remember very clear, one is about the horse. My friend had a horse that she rode a lot, and one day she rode him for a while, and then she said, "You should go ahead and ride him, he's real gentle." I got on the horse, and he took off and headed for the barn. I had to duck or I'd have gotten knocked off as he went through the door. Darlene came in as I got off and convinced me we should try again. She led him to the far end of the pen, and I got on and there he went again, and this time she said, "I know, we'll close the barn door and then you can get a nice ride." We tried it once more, and he didn't go in the barn. He just stood there with his head stuck through the top half of the door that was closed. We finally just gave up on that, so she let me drive the tractor instead. That went much better than the horse.

Another thing was the beautiful flowers they had bloom-ing all over their pasture. They were yellow and so pretty. The day I was going home Darlene's dad took me out to the pasture and helped me dig up a boxful to take home with me. I was so excited, and as soon as Dad came home I had to show him the beautiful flowers that I brought home for him. Dad was the one with the green thumb in our family. The expression on Dad's face when he saw what I had brought home told me something was wrong. As I told you he never got upset, but in a calm voice he explained that they were a bad weed. They were pretty but we had to get rid of them as they would spread all over. I think he called them musk thistles, but anyway, he took them out to our burn barrel and we burned them.

I was staying with my friend, Darlene Soll, for for a few days. I wanted to ride her horse but each time I'd get on he'd go back in the barn so we had to close the barn door. 1956

CHAPTER 40

Playing the Jukebox

During the school year, a new bar and grill went up, and that's where the kids hung out. In time a bowling alley was added. It was called Keeley's, and the last time I was over to Spalding it was still going strong; however, it may have a different name and new owners, but anyway it's still there.

Back in the '50s it cost a dime to play the jukebox, and for those who don't know what a jukebox is, it's like a fancy box with a big window and pretty lights. You put a dime in the slot and then pick a record that you want to hear, push the proper button, and your song plays. There would be maybe forty records, give or take. They had the most popular songs and all the old favorites.

Some of the top songs back then were "Ivory Tower," "Blackboard of My Heart," "Blue Swede Shoes," "Sixteen Ton," "Heart Break Hotel," "I Want You, I Need You, I Love You," "Wayward Winds," "Sweet Old Fashioned Girl," "Shifting Whispering Sands," "When I Lost My Baby," "Dance with Me, Henry," and "Ring of Fire."

CHAPTER 41

Sports in High School

In the summer we had a girls' softball team that I played on. I liked playing softball. I could bat really well. I played left field, I was good at catching, but I never got really good at throwing a long way. The sports we had at school was track, boys' basketball, and girls' volleyball, and also we had boys' baseball and girls' softball. I played on the softball team also. I was very good at volleyball, and I was on the first team all four years in high school and we won a trophy every year.

The game that was the best was the time we played Spalding Academy. This was the Catholic school, and guess who was on that team? My cousin Eleanor Noonan. We didn't ever play them, but this was a tournament and that's the way it worked out, and we were playing for first place. What a game. They were a good team, we were neck and neck the whole game, but in the last few seconds we scored and won the trophy. One of my best memories! This was my senior year we took first in girls' softball and first in volleyball.

Back then schools played teams within forty or fifty miles, and we had the old school bus that really couldn't be trusted to make it there and back, so Dad and Mom would follow it so if they had trouble with it Dad could fix it or go for help. Back then there were no cell phones. Most of the time everything went well. Sometimes I would ride on the bus, but in the winter our car was warmer.

CHAPTER 42

Boys

High school was a lot of fun. You're probably wondering about boys. Well, we had some really cute ones, but they weren't interested in me. At least that's what I thought. I always thought I was fat. I wasn't skinny for sure, but as I look back at my school pictures, I wasn't fat either. I had big bones and I was solid as a rock. Talking about being solid, I loved going into the game at the county fairs where they guessed your weight. I always won that game as they just never got it right.

Well, Ed Bloom became good friends with my brother Don. He was around a lot and in time we started dating. That was when we were in tenth grade. He would take me to the movies, and we would have popcorn and a drink, and after the movie we'd go to Don's Cafe and have hamburgers and milk shakes. Back then all of this would cost less than $5. We dated all through high school.

Back then Spalding had what was called a college inn. It was a big building that was part of a Catholic college or something like that. I guess at one time there were other building there, but this one was all that had survived. It could have been used back then for sports or maybe church services, but anyway, Spalding turned it into a dance hall. Everyone brought their own booze, and a good time was had by all. Ed and I loved dancing, so we would go to dances out there, with the understanding that we'd stay in the building and no drinking. The dance floor was huge and we really had a lot of fun. That is one more thing that is gone from Spalding.

CHAPTER 43

Swimming Pool

Back when I was a seventh, eighth, or ninth grader, Spalding put in a swimming pool. Up until then to get wet you could run under the sprinkler, jump in the river, go up to Pibel Lake, or take a bath, and none of which were as much fun as our new pool. Everyone was taking swimming lessons that first year. Of course, Mom made us take them too as she was afraid of water and she didn't want us to be. The lessons were fun, I really liked the water, and I did really well swimming and even jumping off the diving board. That took me the longest to learn; however, I finally got it figured out and I could even go off the high board and enter the water without hardly a splash. Then I had to be out of the water for a week or more as I got sick. When I came back I just couldn't make a good dive. I don't know why; however, I passed the swimming test with flying colors.

Every day we'd get up and get our chores done so we would have everything done by the time the pool opened in the afternoon. What a good way to keep cool and have fun too. The pool is still there and that's a good thing as there's not too much for kids to do in a small town.

CHAPTER 44

Graduating from High School

H igh school was a good time with studies, sports, plays, dating, proms, and graduations. We also, like they do today, sold things to make money for sneak day. I don't know what they call it now, but back then it was when the seniors took a few days off and went somewhere together, with adults, of course, to keep an eye on us. We went to South Dakota and we had a really good time. Since I could sew, I made my own clothes for the proms and graduation.

Our graduation was on May 15, 1959, and it was held on the stage in front of the gym. We had it all decorated up and chairs set up on the gym floor. After it was over, Mom had a really nice reception for me at our house. I still have all my cards and letters I received and a list of the gifts I got. As I was graduating from high school my brother Don was graduating from eighth grade and into high school the following fall. Since the Marshall kids started going to school at good old Spalding High School, it would be another four years before the Marshall kids wouldn't be there anymore. However, Dad was there for a few more years after Don graduated. Now that us kids were all gone, Mom would go down and help Dad out as much as she could.

The summer after high school went fast. In the fall, Ed, my boyfriend, went off to the army and I went to Omaha to beauty school. This is where this story is going to end.

I thank you for reading my book. I started out writing down things that my children and grandchildren may like to know about someday. I know it would mean so much to me to have this information about my grandparents and my great-grand-parents. Some of my friends and neighbors read some of what I was writing about and talked me into sharing it with others. I hope you enjoyed it. Thanks again. Darlene.

PS. Forgive me if I didn't get something quite right. Remember, these are the memories of a child and sometimes children see things a lot different than an adult.

The Marshall Kids....

November 3, 2016

Roy & Naomi Marshall
December 24, 1964

Darlene was born at Spalding, Nebraska which is in Greeley County. She attended Spalding Public School graduating in May of 1959. Shortly thereafter she married her high school sweetheart, Edward Paul Bloom, who was in the Army. Two weeks later he was shipped to Germany where he spent the next two years. Darlene lived with her parents while he was away and gave birth to their first child, Kenneth Gene. After Edward returned home and as the years flew by children were added to their family Russell Paul, Jeffrey Lynn, Christine Naomi and the last child Dollie Marie, who lived only a short time due to an early birth. In 1980 the couple were divorced. After starting and running a painting business in Grand Island, Nebraska for several years, called "The House Doctors," she met and married Raymond Lloyd Hill in 1993, they ran the business together until they retired and relocated in Scotia, Nebraska in the year 2000. Through the years Darlene has been active in church activities, sold insurance, became a certified wire welder for "Lindsey Manufacturing Company" at Lindsey, Nebraska, being one of the first two women to weld on "Zimmatic Center Pivots." Now she makes Quilts, cares for her flowers, and enjoys fishing with Ray. What she enjoys most is spending time with her four children and their families.

CPSIA information can be obtained
at www.ICGtesting.com
Printed in the USA
FSHW04n1120220318
45822FS